A TACKLE BOX OF

fishing funnies

BOB PHILLIPS
CARTOONS BY JONNY HAWKINS

HARVEST HOUSE™ PUBLISHERS

EUGENE, OREGON

Verses marked KJV are taken from the King James Version of the Bible.

Cover by Terry Dugan Design, Minneapolis, Minnesota

Harvest House Publishers and the author(s) have made every effort to trace the ownership of all poems and quotes. In the event of a question arising from the use of a poem or quote, we regret any error made and will be pleased to make the necessary correction in future editions of this book.

A TACKLE BOX OF FISHING FUNNIES

Text copyright © 2003 by Bob Phillips
Illustration copyright by Jonny Hawkins
Published by Harvest House Publishers
Eugene, Oregon 97402

ISBN 0-7369-1176-6

Printed in the United States of America.

03 04 05 06 07 08 09 10 11 / BC-MS / 10 9 8 7 6 5 4 3 2 1

Do Fish Sleep?

Not really. Fish have periods of inactivity that help their bodies recuperate. Some fish in protected coral reefs can be found leaning against rocks. They might be taking a snooze or just admiring the rocks.

First fisherman: Where do fish with wrinkles go?

Second fisherman: I have no idea.

First fisherman: To the plastic sturgeon.

First fisherman: What do you call a fish without an eye?

Second fisherman: Beats me.

First fisherman: A fsh.

Why don't lobsters share their food with fish?

Because they're shellfish.

It's All in the Family

A juvenile shark is called a cub.

A juvenile whale is called a calf.

A juvenile clam is called a littleneck.

A juvenile eel is called a fry or elver.

A juvenile fish is called a fry, fingerling, minnow, or spawn.

"It it dolphin-safe?"

© 2002 Jonny Hawkins

One fisherman was very successful. Every time he would go fishing he would come home with a huge sack of fish. His reputation for never coming home empty-handed began to grow.

Eventually the news of this great fisherman worked its way to the game warden. Being suspicious and curious, the game warden asked if he could go fishing with him.

The backwoods fisherman agreed with a smile. "Sure," he said. "You're welcome to come to my special lake where I fish."

The game warden arrived early in the morning, and they started out together. However, the warden noticed something very strange. The rural fisherman didn't have a fishing pole; he just carried an old rusty tackle box and a fish net.

After about an hour drive, they arrived at the hidden lake. They got into a boat and rowed out to the center of the lake. Then it happened. The fisherman reached into the rusty tackle box. He pulled out a stick of dynamite, lit it, and tossed it into the lake. As soon as it blew up, a large catch of fish floated to the surface. The fisherman began dipping his net into the water and pulling the fish into the boat.

The game warden was irate. "You can't do that!" he yelled. "It's against the law."

The old fisherman didn't say a word. He just reached into the rusty tackle box and pulled out another stick of dynamite. He lit it and tossed it into the lap of the game warden.

As he smiled, he said, "Are you going to sit there and talk, or are we going to fish?"

First fisherman: How does a fish pay his bills?

Second fisherman: I give up.

First fisherman: With a credit cod.

There are two types of fishermen: those who fish for sport and those who catch something.

Lost and Found

Some sea creatures regenerate parts of their bodies. A starfish can do this along with a crayfish. If a crayfish loses a claw, it grows a replacement one during its next molt. Sometimes the new claw doesn't grow as large as the original one.

What's the difference between a hunter and a fisherman?

A hunter lies in wait, while a fisherman waits and lies.

© 2002 Jonny Hawkins

Special Group Names

A group of goldfish is called troubling.

A group of jellyfish is called smuck or brood.

Minnows have the group name of shoal, steam, or swarm.

Oysters have the group name of bed.

Sardines have the group name of family.

Sharks have the group name of school or shoal.

Trout have the group name of hover.

Two men fishing on Sunday morning were beginning to feel a little guilty, especially because the fish weren't even biting. One of them said to the other, "I guess I should have stayed home and gone to church."

The other angler lazily replied, "I couldn't have gone to church anyway. My wife's home sick in bed."

First fisherman: What do whales like to chew?

Second fisherman: Search me.

First fisherman: Blubbergum.

*Fishing consists of a series
of misadventures interspersed by
occasional moments of glory.*
Howard Marshall

First wife: How was the fishing trip with your husband last weekend?

Second wife: It was terrible. I couldn't do anything right. He said I talked too loud. I moved around too much. I didn't cast the pole the right way. I used the wrong bait, I reeled in too soon...and I caught more fish than he did.

Boy vs. Girl

The way to tell a male lobster from a female lobster is to look at their swimmerets. (These are the forked appendages that the lobsters use for swimming.) On males the spot nearest the solid shell is hard, sharp, and bony. In the females the same area is soft and feathery.

The charm of fishing is that it is elusive but attainable, a perpetual series of occasions for hope.
John Buchan

First Sunday school student: Do you suppose Noah did a lot of fishing from the ark?

Second Sunday school student: How could he? He only had two worms.

I would rather fish than eat, particularly eat fish.
Corey Ford

The great thing about fishing is that it gives you something to do while you're not doing anything.

Coat of Many Colors

A type of dolphin that lives in the Amazon River and the Orinoco River region of South America is called the Pink Dolphin because its skin has a coral color to it.

Nate hooks his first fish.
Grandpa reels in another fisherman.

© 2002 Jonny Hawkins

The cruelest thing you can say to someone fishing in another boat is: "That's a nice fish. May I use it for bait?"

A ten-year-old boy was asked to take care of his younger brother while his parents went shopping. The mother said, "Why don't you take Willard fishing with you?" The ten-year-old was not too happy but agreed.

When his parents arrived home, the older boy said: "Don't ever ask me to take Willard fishing with me again."

"Why?" asked his mother. "Did he make too much noise?"

"No," said the boy.

"Did he scare the fish by playing in the water?" asked his father.

"No," said the boy. "I couldn't catch any fish because Willard ate all the bait!"

Now, who can solve my problem,
and grant my lifelong wish?
Are fishermen all big liars?
Or do only liars fish?

Anonymous

Smile

As everyone knows, sharks have several rows of teeth. If a tooth in the front row is lost, the one behind it grows in to take its place. It is estimated that in a ten-year period a tiger shark will replace as many as 24,000 teeth.

A stranger stopped his car to watch the strange behavior of a fisherman on a riverbank. First the fisherman hooked a

© 2002 Jonny Hawkins

big pike but threw it back into the water. Then he landed a beautiful, large trout. He threw it back into the water also. It wasn't long before he reeled in a small bluegill. With a smile he put it into his fish bag.

The stranger couldn't take it any longer. He interrupted the fisherman and asked, "Why did you throw back the big pike and the large trout and only keep the small bluegill?"

"Small frying pan," the fisherman replied.

First fisherman: What fish is a household pet?

Second fisherman: I give up.

First fisherman: A catfish.

As Great Britain was being attacked by the Germans during World War II, Winston Churchill made a comment to the French people, during one of his radio broadcasts. He said, "We are waiting for the long-promised German invasion. So are the fishes."

You Give Me a Charge, Baby

Electric eels can produce charges that average 350 volts. Some eels have had voltage go as high as 550 volts.

The eels can repeat this shock up to 150 times per hour.

"Can we take Spunky with us since he has worms?"

© 2002 Jonny Hawkins

Bait the hook well; this fish will bite.
William Shakespeare

Two fishermen were looking for a new fishing area. As they were driving down a dirt road in the mountains, they found a sign that said: "Road to Lake Clear Water closed." There were two logs blocking the road.

They decided to explore and find the lake and try out a new spot. They hooked a chain around the end of one log and pulled it out of the way. They then proceeded down the old, bumpy road in their pickup truck. The two men enjoyed the beautiful scenery and talked of fish.

About ten miles into the journey they came to a landslide that completely blocked the road. They had to turn around and drive back to the main dirt road.

As they arrived back at the main road they noticed a hand-written note on the backside of the sign that said "Road to Lake Clear Water closed." It read: "When are you ever going to learn to believe signs?"

Spouting Off

Whales do not spout water. The whale's blowhole is its nostril. Air is forced out causing any water on the top of the whale to spray.

First fisherman: Why do whales paint their flippers different colors?

Second fisherman: It's beyond me.

First fisherman: So they can hide in jellybean jars.

Second fisherman: I've never seen a whale in a jellybean jar.

First fisherman: See how good they hide?

How Many?

How many kinds of fish are there? One estimate suggests more than 30,000!

First fisherman: Do you like shows about fish?

Second fisherman: Yeah, they really hook me.

Why do some fishermen use helicopters
to get their bait?

The whirly bird gets the worm.

First fisherman: What do you call a man
who goes fishing all the time?

Second fisherman: I give up.

First fisherman: Rod.

Stranger: Did you catch any fish today?

Fisherman: Yep, I did. I took 43 out of
the lake this morning.

Stranger: Do you know who I am?

Fisherman: Nope.

Stranger: I'm the game warden.

Fisherman: Do you know who I am?

Stranger: Nope.

Fisherman: I'm the biggest liar in three
counties.

What is the squid's favorite television program?

Whale of Fortune.

There is no use in your walking five miles to fish when you can depend on being just as unsuccessful near home.

Mark Twain

What's in a Name?

A male whale is called a bull, and a female whale is called a cow.

Customer: Your sign says, *"Any sandwich you can name."* I would like a whale sandwich.

Waiter: Okay. [He soon returns from the kitchen.] I'm afraid I can't get you a whale sandwich.

Customer: Why not? Your sign says *"Any sandwich."*

Waiter: The cook says he doesn't want to start a new whale for one lousy sandwich.

Fisherman's wife: Do you have any more
of those small plastic floats?

Fisherman: Why do you ask?

Fisherman's wife: The one you gave me
keeps sinking.

"Will you quit splashing and scaring them off?"

© 2002 Jonny Hawkins

First fisherman: What is the best way to get in touch with a fish?

Second fisherman: I couldn't guess.

First fisherman: Drop him a line.

"Could you wrap this for me?
It's for the missus...it's our anniversary."

© 2002 Jonny Hawkins

The Sky is Falling

Fish have fallen from the sky on numerous occasions. One such event took place near Killarney Station in Australia's Northern Territory. During the month of February in 1974, approximately 150 perchlike fish dropped from the sky during a tropical storm. It is believed that some form of whirlwind created a waterspout effect and sucked the fish out of the water, later depositing them on the ground.

Why are dolphins smarter than humans?
It only takes dolphins about three hours to train people to stand at the side of a pool and feed them fish.

Fishing is generally best before you get there and after you leave.

For many years a certain white whale and a tiny herring had been inseparable friends. Wherever the white whale roamed in search of food, the herring was sure to be swimming right along beside him.

One fine spring day the herring turned up off the coast of Nova Scotia without his companion. Naturally all the other fish were curious. A sea bass finally asked the herring what happened to his friend the white whale.

"How should I know?" the herring replied. "Am I my blubber's kipper?"

First fisherman: How do you make a slow whale fast?

Second fisherman: I have no clue.

First fisherman: Don't feed him.

I make it a rule never to weigh or measure a fish I've caught, but simply to estimate its dimensions as accurately as possible, and then, when telling about it, to improve those figures by roughly a fifth, or 20 percent. I do this mainly because most people believe all fishermen

*exaggerate by at least 20 percent, and so
I allow for the discounting my audience is
almost certain to apply.*
Ed Zern

Lion King

Lionfish are very beautiful to behold. They
have a fragile-looking plumage. Within
this plumage are 18 venom-tipped spines.
If a human touched one of these spines he
or she could be immediately knocked out,
have a drop in blood pressure, and die.

First fisherman: I caught a 450-pound
marlin the other day.

Second fisherman: That's nothing. I was
fishing off the coast of Florida last
month and hooked a lamp from an old
Spanish galleon. In fact, when I pulled
it up the old lamp was still lit.

First fisherman: If you will blow out the
light, I'll take 250 pounds off the
marlin.

Do the Lobster Dance!

In the fall of the year on the Bimini Islands
in the Bahamas, spiny lobsters migrate
from the reefs to deep water. They do this

by forming marching columns of up to 50 lobsters. Each lobster hooks a pair of its front legs around the tail of the lobster in front. They then move as a group across the sea bed at a rate as fast as a man can swim.

© 2002 Jonny Hawkins

First fisherman: What lives at the bottom of the sea, is brightly colored, and is very popular around Easter time?

Second fisherman: You've got me guessing.

First fisherman: An oyster egg.

Catching Fish with Your Toes

Children in Thailand are often found in the rice paddies catching small fish with their toes.

A preacher who was an ardent fisherman performed a wedding. He asked the groom, "Do you promise to love, honor, and cherish this woman?"

"I do," answered the groom.

Then turning to the bride, he said, "Okay, reel him in."

What is the appropriate material for a fisherman to wear?

Fishnet.

"Michael got a hook caught in his ear 4 years ago
at summer camp, and decided to go with the look."

© 2002 Jonny Hawkins

*A man can become so caught
up in fishing that it actually
becomes a grim business.*
Sparse Grey Hackle

The definition of an optimist is a
fisherman who takes a camera with him
when he goes fishing.

The determined angler staggered up to
the counter with an armload of the latest
gear. As the cashier was ringing up the
total, which came to several hundred
dollars, the angler commented, "You know,
you could save me an awful lot of money
if you'd just start selling fish here."

An honest fisherman is a pretty
uninteresting person.

"How many fish have you caught?" asked a man as he watched an older angler fish from the pier.

"Well," said the older man, "if I catch this one I'm after and then catch two more, I'll have three."

"Hang on, Marty, it's a fight of a lifetime!!"
Yee Hawwwwwwwwww!!

© 2002 Jonny Hawkins

*Your bait of falsehood takes the Carp
of truth, and thus do we . . .
by indirections find directions out.*

Shakespeare

Man-Eating Fish

The piranha is the most ferocious fresh-water fish. Piranhas are found in the rivers of South America. They are attracted by blood and, as a group, can completely strip an animal within a few minutes.

Three hundred people were reportedly eaten at one time when an overloaded riverboat capsized. This event took place in the Brazilian port of Obidos on September 19, 1981.

A sporting goods store had just put up a large display of expensive fishing tackle. A customer picked up one of the newest lures and inspected the gleaming metal and colorful plastic.

"Do the fish really go for these things?" he asked the salesperson.

"Dunno," replied the clerk. "We don't sell 'em to the fish."

Ed reels in a perfectly nice panfish.

© 2002 Jonny Hawkins

*Fishermen are born honest,
but they get over it.*
Ed Zern

*All good fisherman stay young
until they die, for fishing
is the only dream of youth that
doth not grow stale with age.*
J.W. Muller

What's blue and red all over?

A sunburned whale. (Whales really can
get sunburned!)

Sounds Fishy

Many fish emit sounds. The singing toad-fish hums. The male oyster toadfish whis-tles. The electric catfish hisses. The horse mackerel grunts like a pig. The trunkfish and puffers growl like dogs. Fish known as drums creak, hum, purr, and whistle loudly.

The way to solve the noise problem is to go and catch them.

What kind of a fish do you find in a bird cage?

Perch.

"I'll have crickets, night crawlers and a side of flies...and supersize it!"

© 2002 Jonny Hawkins

Unfortunately fish seem to go on vacation the same time we do.

First fisherman: What is the most valuable fish in the water?

Second fisherman: I have no idea.

First fisherman: The goldfish.

What plays the piano and works for Chicken of the Sea?

The piano-tuna.

Why did the fish go on a diet?

It weighed too much for its scales.

Don't Give Up

Bob Ploegar holds the Guinness record for the longest fight with a fish on a rod and reel. His battle lasted 32 hours and 5 minutes.

Sitting still and wishing
Made no person great;
The good Lord sends the fishing,
But you must dig the bait.

...[I'm] spending more time with my fly firmly attached to the branches of trees and almost none of it attached to the lips of the trout.

Tom Sutcliffe

If 20 sharks swim after one fisherman,
 what time is it?

Twenty after one.

Meat is murder,
but fish is justifiable homicide.
Jeremy Hardy

© 2002 Jonny Hawkins

High-Flying Fish

Various animals have been sent into space
or on low-level rocket launches. Among
these animals have been jellyfish.

© 2002 Jonny Hawkins

A merchant decided to open his own business selling fish. He took great pains in painting his first sign that read, "FRESH FISH SOLD HERE."

It wasn't long before one of his customers said, "I know you are an honest merchant. You would never sell anything but the freshest fish. Because of that you ought to change your sign to read 'FISH SOLD HERE.'" The merchant followed the customer's advice.

A week later another customer remarked, "You know, it is unnecessary to use the word 'Here' in your sign. I suggest you just say, 'FISH FOR SALE.'" The merchant followed the customer's advice and changed his sign.

Within a few days another customer said, "I've been studying your sign. I think that everyone knows you are not giving fish away. You don't need the words 'For Sale' in your sign. All you have to have is a sign that just says "FISH.'" The merchant followed the customer's advice and ended up with a sign that only had one word.

Finally, another customer said, "You know, you don't have to use the word 'FISH' in your sign. Everyone in the neigh-borhood can smell the fish a block away. They know you are selling fish. All they have to do is follow their noses." The merchant followed the customer's advice and removed any advertising about fish.

The next day, all of his customers went across the street to a store that had a sign that read: "FRESH FISH SOLD HERE."

Twit

The term "twit" is the technical name for a pregnant goldfish. It is also a name for a not-so-bright individual.

© 2002 Jonny Hawkins

First fisherman: What lives in the sea,
   has eight legs, and is quick on the
   draw?

Second fisherman: Beats me.

First fisherman: Billy the Squid.

I never lost a little fish—
Yes, I am free to say.
It always was the biggest fish
I caught, that got away.
   Eugene Field

Bragging may not bring happiness, but
no man having caught a large fish goes
home through an alley.

What's blue and lumpy and comes in a
   can?

Cream of Whale soup.

The Tale of the Duck-Eating Monster

For years there was a story of a duck-eating monster located in Lake Washington, Seattle. On November 5, 1987, people found the monster. It was a dead fish that washed ashore. The fish was a sturgeon that weighed 900 pounds and was 11 feet long. Washington State fisheries official Tony Floor estimated that it was 80 years of age. Although they don't eat ducks, sturgeons have been known to live to 100 years of age and to grow to more than 20 feet long.

Fishing is a delusion entirely surrounded by liars in old clothes.
Don Marquis

Once upon a time there was a fisherman who had two sons named Toward and Away. Every day he would go fishing and return late at night. He would always talk to his family about the giant fish he almost caught. One day he took Toward and Away fishing with him.

That night he returned home more excited than ever.

"Today's sermon is about Jesus separating himself from the crowd and going out into the boat. And now I'm going to be like Jesus."

© 2002 Jonny Hawkins

"Clarabelle," he said to his wife, "you should have seen the fish I saw today! It was a tremendous gray fish, 12 feet long. It had horns and fur all over its back. It had legs like a caterpillar. On top of that, it crawled out of the water, snatched our son Toward, and swallowed him in one gulp!"

"Good gracious!" exclaimed Clarabelle. "That's horrible!"

"Oh, that was nothing," said her husband, the fisherman. "You should have seen the one that got Away."

"That was Ronelle's first time at baiting her own hook."

© 2002 Jonny Hawkins

Where do you take a squid that is very sick?

To the doctopus.

The Traveling Toadfish

The longest recorded journey of a sea creature was more than three million miles. This great journey was accomplished by two oyster toadfish on Discovery space shuttle mission STS-95. We don't know if they got space sick during their wild ride.

Why does the ocean roar?

You would, too, if you had lobsters in your bed.

After fishing for trout all day and not catching any, a fisherman in Colorado packed up his boat and gear and drove home. On the way he passed a fish market. He turned his car around and went back to the market.

He went inside and noticed they had ten very large trout for sale. The fisherman asked the man behind the counter to throw the fish to him.

"Why do you want me to throw the fish to you?" asked the salesperson.

"Because I'm going to catch them. I may be a lousy fisherman, but I'm not a liar."

There is certainly something in angling... that tends to produce a gentleness of spirit and a pure serenity of mind.
Washington Irving

Brain Power

The brain of sperm whales can weigh more than 20 pounds. The head of a whale can contain up to 500 gallons of pure oil.

Angler's motto: I only fish on days that end in "Y."

Young Charlie went fishing with his father one Saturday. Upon arriving home the boy ran into the house crying. His mother asked what was wrong.

The boy began to explain what happened. "Dad and I were fishing when all of a sudden Dad caught a giant bass. He fought it for almost half an hour. As he reeled it to the boat, the fish line snagged on the motor and broke. The large fish got away."

"You shouldn't be crying about that. I've taught you to laugh things off when something goes bad. It was an accident. You need to learn to make a joke about it."

"But that's what I did."

Why do you think dolphins have wrinkles?

Have you ever tried to iron one?

Why didn't the baby trout go to lunch with the stork?

He was afraid he'd get stuck with the bill.

Do Fish Climb Trees?

The climbing perch of South Asia has accomplished this trick. It can live out of water for short periods of time. It moves along on its mudskippers and has been found climbing palm trees. The climbing perch holds on using its pectoral fins. Maybe it's looking for coconuts?

© 2002 Jonny Hawkins

The wife of an avid fisherman was tired of him being gone every weekend on a fishing trip. She decided they needed a vacation together. She drug him to Europe to travel and see the sights.

Upon arriving home the avid fisherman was asked by his friends how he liked traveling through Europe. He said that most of it was okay—he could put up with it. They asked him what he liked most. Was it Rome? Was it the Swiss Alps? Was it the Eiffel Tower?

The fisherman replied, "I liked Venice the best. I could sit in my hotel room and fish right out the window."

First fisherman: What's stranger than seeing a catfish?

Second fisherman: What can it be?

First fisherman: Seeing a goldfish bowl.

First fisherman: What did the fish say when he was caught on the hook?

Second fisherman: I give up.

First fisherman: Gosh! I thought I knew
all the angles.

The Pygmy

The smallest fish is the dwarf pygmy
goby. It measures 0.35 inches long.

How far a fisherman
stretches the truth depends
on the length of his arms.

First fisherman: Did you mark that place
where the fishing was good? We'll want
to come back to that spot.

Second fisherman: Yep, I put an X on the
side of the boat.

First fisherman: That was sure stupid.
What if we take out a different boat
next time?

Tongue twister: The small, shiny silver
sign signifies sharks swimming.

*I waded to shore where I sat
and considered the inconsistency
of anglers in general and
the dumbness of one in particular.*

Ray Bergman

A Fishy Deception

In the Indian Ocean several scientists were observing a large school of finger-size fish when a barracuda approached.

The school of fish drew close together and created a formation that resembled a large shark or dolphin. They seemed to move as a unit, creating the impression of being a single, large fish. The barracuda immediately turned and left at the sight of the "larger" fish.

Where do jellyfish get their jelly?
From ocean currents.

Octopus: Why are you swimming so near the surface of the water?

Little fish: I'm in high school now.

First fisherman: What's the difference between a girl whale and a boy whale?

Second fisherman: I have no idea.

First fisherman: One sings soprano and the other sings bass.

*Angling may be said to be
so like mathematics that it
can never fully be learnt.*
Izaak Walton

High-Society Fish

The most valuable fish in the world is the Russian sturgeon. In 1924, a female sturgeon weighing 2,706 pounds was pulled ashore. It yielded 540 pounds of the finest Russian caviar worth $289,000.

"What kinda bait you usin'?"

© 2002 Jonny Hawkins

Three-fourths of the earth's surface is water and one-fourth is land. It stands to reason that the good Lord intended for man to spend three times as much time fishing as he does plowing.

Diner: I don't like this piece of cod. It's not half as good as the one I ate here three weeks ago.

Waiter: I have no idea what is wrong. It should be just as good. It's the other half of the same fish.

TELE-FISHIN'

© 2002 Jonny Hawkins

There were lots of people who committed
crimes during the year who would not
have done so if they had been fishing,
and I assure you that the increase
in crime is due to a lack of those qualities
of mind and character which impregnate
the soul of every fisherman except
those who get no bites.

Herbert Hoover

Diner: Waiter, this fish is bad.

Waiter: You naughty fish, you!

Underwater Music

Dolphins have no vocal cords but commu-
nicate with each other using sounds. This
is done by forcing air through their blow-
holes. Dolphins can emit at least 32 different sounds. These include whistles, groans,
barks, clicks, and squeals.

Whales also seem to converse with one
another by making whistles and chirps.
The song of the humpback whale can last
up to 30 minutes. Their sounds can be
very loud, going up to 188 decibels. This
is louder than a jet plane. The moans of
fin whales have been picked up as much as
100 miles away.

First fisherman: Where did the thief
  wind up for stealing oysters?

Second fisherman: I don't have the foggiest.

First fisherman: Small clams court.

Some people insist that a fishing pole
is a stick with a worm on both ends of it.

© 2002 Jonny Hawkins

Two fishermen were sitting on a bridge with their lines in the water. They agreed to make a bet on who'd be the first one to catch a fish. One of the men soon got a bite and became so excited that he fell off the bridge.

"That's not fair!" said the other fisherman. "If you're going to dive for them, the bet's off."

Eating an anchovy
is like eating an eyebrow.

Get Ready for Dinner

Are you aware that moray eels can grow up to 12 feet in length? According to historic records eels seemed to be an esteemed delicacy. In one special dinner it is stated that Caesar served 6,000 moray eels as the main course.

How do you make a whale sandwich?
First of all you get a very large loaf of bread. . . .

A fisherman was arrested by the game warden for catching 25 more trout than the law allowed.

"Guilty or not guilty?" asked the judge.

"Guilty," said the fisherman.

"That will be a fine of $250," said the judge.

After the fisherman paid the fine he had one request. "Your honor, I'd respectfully like to ask for several copies of the court record."

The judge was surprised. "What do you want the copies for?"

"I want to show all my fishing friends."

I got a lot of bites while I was fishing last weekend.

One of them was even a fish.

The only time a fisherman
tells the truth is when
he calls another fisherman a liar.

Odor in the Court

There is one recorded case of a wife in Newfoundland who asked for a divorce because of her husband's unusual affection for pets.

The husband insisted on keeping a large catfish in their bathtub.

The divorce was granted. Sounds a little fishy doesn't it?

"Care for some wine with your cheese bait?"

© 2002 Jonny Hawkins

Did you hear about the new invention?
It is a fishhook designed with a small
underwater camera on it. It was invented
by a fisherman to take pictures of the
fish that got away.

What's as big as a whale and doesn't
   weigh anything?
A whale's shadow.

*We may say of angling as Dr. Boteler
said of strawberries: "Doubtless God
could have made a better berry,
but doubtless God never did."*

*And so, (if I might be judge) God
never did make a more calm, quiet,
innocent recreation than angling.*

Izaak Walton

Take your boy fishing,
and you won't have to hunt for him.

A fisherman digging a hole in his backyard was found by his next door neighbor.

"What are you doing?"

"My goldfish died and I'm digging him a grave."

"That's a very big hole for a small gold-fish."

"That's because he is inside your cat."

"There's no action I tell you. None whatsoever."

© 2002 Jonny Hawkins

One Big Bowl of Clam Chowder

The quahog is a marine clam. It measures from three to five inches long, and it can live up to 200 years of age.

Game warden: Fishing?

Man without a license: No, drowning worms.

"And the motion passes 5 to 4
that we attract those wayward fishermen
by stocking the baptistry with bass."

© 2002 Jonny Hawkins

Statistics show that for the first 20 years of a fisherman's life, his mother asks him where he is going. For the next 40 years, his wife asks him where he is going. At the fisherman's funeral, all of the mourners ask the same question.

First fisherman: What fish is man's best friend?
Second fisherman: Who knows?
First fisherman: The dogfish.

That's Some Fishing Trip

Dave Romeo holds the Guinness record for catching bass: He caught 3,001 bass in 77 days.

*Any man who can swap horses
or catch fish, and not lie about it,
is just about as pious as men ever
get to be in this world.*
Josh Billings

First fisherman: Why is that guy over there throwing his fishing line up into the air?

Second fisherman: He must be fly fishing.

An avid fisherman decided to go ice fishing. It was a bitterly cold winter day when he cut a hole in the ice. He was there for several hours and didn't catch a thing.

Then the fisherman noticed a small boy who came to the lake. He cut a hole in the ice and proceeded to catch one fish after the other.

The fisherman couldn't stand it any longer. He went over to the boy and said, "What's your secret? I've been here for hours and haven't caught a thing."

The boy replied, "Roo raf roo reep ra rurms rarm."

"I'm sorry," said the fisherman. "I didn't catch that."

"Roo raf roo reep ra rurms rarm," said the boy.

"I'm sorry, but I cannot understand a word you are saying."

The boy then spat out a wad of ugly slime into his two hands. "I said, you have to keep the worms warm."

Shocking News

The Portuguese man-of-war is a slimy type of jellyfish. It has long tentacles that can be up to 60 feet in length. It has a very bad sting for humans. The pain can be severe, blood pressure will drop, and often the victim will go into shock. Some people have been known to die from the sting. There is no known antidote.

"I'd like to relocate from the river, but I don't want to be ex-stream."

© 2002 Jonny Hawkins

First fisherman: What do little swordfish learn in school?

Second fisherman: You tell me.

First fisherman: Their ABSeas.

"You're under arrest, too sir—
for aiding and a'baiting."

© 2002 Jonny Hawkins

It's always the big ones that get away. That's because a fisherman's eyes are bigger than his hooks.

Why wasn't the woman swimmer afraid of the shark?

Because it was a man-eating shark.

First fisherman: Who snatched the baby squid and held it for ransom?

Second fisherman: I can't guess.

First fisherman: Squidnappers.

The new minister of the church was a little upset with Mr. Johnson. "I hear that you went to the football game instead of coming to church this morning."

"That's not true, pastor. And here is the string of fish to prove it."

*Perhaps fishing is, for me,
only an excuse to be near rivers.*
Roderick L. Haig-Brown

"Have you had a bite yet?"

© 2002 Jonny Hawkins

Different Strokes for Different Fish

Fish like the blue marlin, manta rays, and bluefin tuna swim from the ocean surface to a depth of about 600 feet. Fish like the oarfish, the hatchet fish, and the lantern fish swim at a level of 600 to 3,000 feet in the ocean. Fish like the tripod fish, the rattail, and the deep sea angler swim at a depth of 3,000 feet or more.

To go fishing is the chance to wash one's soul with pure air, with the rush of the brook or the serenity of a lake, and the shimmer of the sun on blue water. It brings meekness and inspiration from the decency of nature, charity toward tackle-makers, patience toward fish, a mockery of profits and egos, a quieting of hate, a rejoicing that you do not have to decide a darned thing until next week. And it is a discipline in the equality of men— for all men are equal before fish.

Herbert Hoover

Two elderly men went fishing one morning. They sat in the boat for hours and said nothing to each other while their lines were in the water. After a while one of them shuffled his legs a little, trying to work out a cramp in his leg. About three hours later he shuffled his legs again.

Finally the other elderly fisherman looked up at him and said, "Did you come here to fish or to practice your dancing?"

"Remember what you've said about fish hiding in the shadows...?"

© 2002 Jonny Hawkins

*Presidents have only two moments
of personal seclusion. One is in prayer;
the other is fishing—and they
cannot pray all the time!*
Herbert Hoover

Do All Fish Lay
Their Eggs in the Water?

The answer is no. The grunions didn't want to go along with the plan. In the coastal waters of California and Mexico, the grunions lay their eggs in the spring of the year. These silver fish ride the waves onto the sandy beaches. The males and females swim together and mix their sperm and eggs, then bury the fertilized eggs in the sand. They take the next wave back out to the ocean.

First fisherman: What do you get when you put giant fish in your living room?

Second fisherman: My mind is blank.

First fisherman: Whale-to-whale carpeting.

An avid fisherman was fishing in a river for trout. He was dressed in the latest fishing outfit; he had the best fishing gear. He was feeling very good about himself. A young country boy was sitting on the bank of the river watching him.

Suddenly, the fisherman got a bite and pulled out a very large trout. Smiling, he turned to the young boy and said, "Did you ever have a trout this size at your home?"

"Nope," said the boy quietly. "My father always throws the little ones back in."

Only the Classics

In 1985, 3,000 beluga (white whales) were trapped in an ice flow. This took place in the Senyavina Strait. The Russian government sent an ice-breaking ship called the Moskva to help rescue the stranded whales. The Moskva opened a 70-foot wide pathway to freedom but the whales didn't escape. They seemed to be afraid of the ship and would not follow it to open waters. The Russians tried everything they knew to get the whales to follow them but it was to no avail. They began to experiment with various types of sounds. They even tried jazz and popular music. They finally were successful when they began to play classical music from the loud speakers of the ship. Whales must not be into hard rock or rap music.

A fisherman and a skin diver were out in a boat together. They were fishing over a man-made reef near a coastal bay. The fisherman's line got hooked on something, and he couldn't reel in. "I bet I got hooked on one of those old cars they put into the reef."

The skin diver said, "I'll bet you got hold of one of those huge redfish. I'll dive in and shoot him with my spear gun."

After about a half an hour the skin diver appeared on the surface.

"What took you so long?" said the fisherman.

"I ran out of oxygen and spears." Exhausted, the skin diver climbed into the boat. "Every time I get a clear shot at that redfish, it rolls up the window."

Fishing is not a matter of life and death. It is much more important than that.

What's in a Name

There is a fish called the guppy. It is a freshwater fish found in the West Indies and the northern part of South America. They were named after R.J. Lechmer Guppy.

"Man! There goes another big one that got away!"

© 2002 Jonny Hawkins

A fisherman and his wife went to a lake to fish. They were in the boat for a while when the wife noticed her husband looking at her in a very loving manner.

"What are you thinking about?" she asked.

"Oh," he replied, "I was just thinking what great lures your earrings would make."

Trout are quite unaware
of their exalted status.
Harold Blaisdell

Why did the whale lie in the road with his flippers in the air?

He wanted to trip the birds.

Fishing simply sent me out of my mind.
I could neither think nor talk of

anything else, so that mother was angry and said that she would not let me fish again because I might fall ill from such excitement.

Sergei Aksakov

"Aren't you overdoing it a bit with your secret fishing spot?"

© 2002 Jonny Hawkins

How Do Antarctic Fish Survive the Cold?

Fish in the Antarctic have a substance in their bodies called glycoprotein. It works similar to the antifreeze we put into our cars. If they did not have this in their system, they would freeze.

"I told you those fish had a lot of fight in 'em."

© 2002 Jonny Hawkins

Knock, knock.
Who's there?
Halibut.
Halibut who?
Halibut a kiss, sweetie?

It is against the law to catch fish in some
   waters and a miracle in others.

What does the story of Jonah and the
   great fish teach us?
You can't keep a good man down.

Two fishermen went on a fishing trip in
the Amazon. They were fishing from a
dock while dangling their feet in the
water. Suddenly an alligator bit off one
of the toes of one of the fishermen.
   "An alligator just bit off some of my
toe!" yelled the first fisherman.
   The second one replied, "Which one?"

"How should I know," said the angler, pulling his foot from the water. "All alligators look alike to me."

Jaws

The black swallower has jaws that are on hinges. This enables them to swallow fish twice their own size. The swallower's stomach will stretch to take on this large catch.

What do you call a huge whale with a large vocabulary?

Moby Dicktionary.

Two city slickers went ice-fishing in Minnesota. When they got back to camp, the man in the bait shop asked, "Did you catch many fish?"

"Heck no," said one of the city slickers. "It took us seven hours to get the boat into the water."

A very famous Alaskan hunting guide changed his business and became a fishing guide. When he was asked why, he replied, "Well, nobody has mistaken me for a fish yet."

Work is for people
who do not know how to fish.

Why did the dolphin paint its head yellow?
It wanted to see if blondes have more fun.

"Giddyap"

The slowest fish is the sea horse. It only moves approximately .001 miles per hour. That would be about 5 feet in one hour.

*With the exception of painting,
nothing in this life has held my interest
as much as fishing. Fishing with a fly,
bait, a handline; I don't much care.
Fishing, in my estimation, is not a hobby,
a diversion, a pastime, a sport,
an interest, a challenge, or an escape.
It is a necessary passion.*
Russell Chatham

"Sorry. Mr. Henderson is busy
on another line right now."

© 2002 Jonny Hawkins

First fisherman: What happens when you ask an oyster a personal question?

Second fisherman: It's unknown to me.

First fisherman: It clams up.

First goldfish: So I guess you're not dating that terrific-looking lobster anymore.

Second goldfish: It didn't work out. He was too shellfish.

Spinners and Spotters

A spotted dolphin can jump as high as 20 feet above the surface of the water. Spinner dolphins have the ability to leap from the water and spin at the same time. They have been known to make seven or more complete turns in a single leap.

Who was the strongest man in the Bible?

Jonah. Even the huge fish couldn't keep him down.

Game warden: Hey, you're not allowed to fish here!

Fisherman: I am not fishing. I'm teaching my worm to swim.

An angler was fishing in the Amazon River when his boat capsized. He noticed a native walking on the shore. The fisherman yelled to him, "Are there any alligators in the water?"

The native stopped, turned, and said, "There are no alligators in the water."

Relieved, the fisherman started to splash toward shore. Along the way the fisherman again yelled at the native. "Are you sure there are no alligators in these waters?"

"I'm sure," replied the native. "The piranhas ate them all."

Talk About a Fish Out of Water

The mudskipper is a four-inch fish with goggle eyes. It is found in the swamps of Southeast Asia. The mudskipper has a reputation for climbing trees. In fact, it spends almost half of its time out of water. Before it crawls out on the land it fills its gill chambers with air and water so it can spend several hours at a time out of the water. It climbs trees by the use of suckers attached to its fins. Two other fish from Southeast Asia also spend a lot of time out of the water. The first is the climbing perch and the other is the walking catfish. Maybe they heard about a fish fry and wanted to attend?

The way most fisherman catch fish is by the tale.

A country lad, observing a city fisher-man on the bank of a stream, asked, "How many fish ya got mister?"

"None, yet," was the response.

"That ain't bad," said the boy. "There was a feller who fished here for two weeks, and he didn't get any more than you got in half an hour!"

"There's a small net near you..."

© 2002 Jonny Hawkins

First fisherman: I caught a gigantic fish the other day. It was a real monster.

Second fisherman: I saw a picture of your fish. It was only eight inches long.

First fisherman: That is true. But a fish can lose a lot of weight in the battle to catch and reel him in.

Fighting Fish

The male Siamese fighting fish from Thailand guard their young with such vigor that they are used in gambling similar to "fighting" cocks.

What is big, famous, and spouts water?
The Prince of Whales.

Whale Suicide

Whales sometimes beach themselves and cannot get back into the ocean. Some scientists believe this event occurs when the whales sense they are dying. The largest event of mass whale suicide took place in New Zealand in 1974. Seventy-two giant sperm whales swam ashore and died on the beach.

There were three men fishing in a boat halfway across a lake. The first man suddenly said, "I forgot my lunch." He got out of the boat and walked to shore on top of the water. He got his lunch out of the car and came back walking on top of the water.

Later, the second man said, "I forgot my fishing tackle." He too got out of the boat and walked on top of the water to shore. Soon he returned walking on top of the water with his tackle box in his hand.

By this time, the third man thought to himself, *They're not going to outsmart me.* He turned to the others and said, "I forgot my bait can." He then got out of the boat to walk across the water. He immediately sank.

The first man said to the second, "Maybe we should have told him where the stepping-stones are."

Atheist: Do you honestly believe that Jonah spent three days and three nights in the belly of a great fish?

Preacher: I don't know for sure, sir, but when I get to heaven I'll ask him.

Atheist: But suppose he isn't in heaven?

Preacher: Then you ask him!

Two fishermen were discussing last year's hunting and fishing successes. The topper came when one fellow said, "My buddy and I went duck hunting. A nice flock of mallards came over this pond, and would you believe that with one shot I got my limit of five ducks!

"Not having a dog, I put on my waders and went out to get them. The water was a little deep and spilled over into my waders. When I came back to shore with my ducks and emptied out my waders, I discovered that I also had my limit of fish!"

"Baited Yo-Yo"

© 2002 Jonny Hawkins

Fishermen's Prayer

God grant that I may live to fish until my
    dying day
And when my final cast is made
And life has slipped away,
I pray that God's great landing net
Will catch me in its sweep,
And in His mercy
God will judge me big enough to keep.

Sleepy Time

Do dolphins sleep? If you said, "Yes," you
were half right. Dolphins need to breathe
and surface about every two minutes to
get air. If they didn't they would suffocate.

So when do they sleep?

Dolphins have brains with two hemispheres. Eight hours a day these two
hemispheres are awake at the same time.
During the next eight hours only the left
hemisphere sleeps. During the last eight
hours the right hemisphere sleeps. In this
way they can slowly continue to swim and
breathe and be semi-alert.

First fisherman: Who delivers Easter
    treats to all the fish in the sea?
Second fisherman: How should I know?
First fisherman: The Oyster Bunny.

He caught a fish so big that the negative weighed five pounds.

*The art of bottom fishing
is that of letting the fish
come to the fisherman,
instead of vice versa. . . .
Bottom fishing, in short,
is the thinking man's fishing.*

Louis D. Rubin

First fisherman: What is a shark's favorite game?

Second fisherman: How should I know?

First fisherman: Salmon Says.

Anyone for Lobster?

The state of Maine harvests more lobsters than any other state. They catch 47 million pounds each year, which generates approximately $137 million in revenue.

Did you hear the one about the electric eel? It's shocking.

The Angler's Special Prayer

Give me, O Lord, to catch a fish
So large that even I,
In boasting of it afterwards,
Shall have no need to lie.

Allan M. Laing

© 2002 Jonny Hawkins

Do fish bite at sunrise?

No, they bite at flies and worms.

Correction

*In last week's paper we ran a story about a
local man who injured himself while fishing.
This was an error. We have since learned
that it didn't happen while he was fishing.
He dislocated his shoulders the next day
while describing a fish that got away.*

Ron Dentinger

Why did the whale sit on a red cherry?

*So his flipper wouldn't get into the
chocolate sundae.*

So Much for Ecology

People who think they understand ecology
are sometimes misguided. In 1960, some
ecologists thought it would be good to add
Nile perch to Lake Victoria, Africa's largest
lake. They surmised that it would add
available protein for the local inhabitants.

The perch had a different mind. They
ate all of the other 300 species of fish in
the lake.

Don't Ye Talk to Me of Work!

I'm jest goin' fishin'
Where the speckled beauties lurk,
'Round the pools a-swishin'
Ne'er a thought have I of care,
Settin' on a green bank there,
Drinkin' in the soft June air,
Void of all ambition!

"Fly Fishing"

© 2002 Jonny Hawkins

Wife: My husband just sits in the living room fishing in a bucket of water in the middle of the room.

Friend: That is strange. Are you going to take him to the psychiatrist?

Wife: I would, but we really need the fish.

"You should have seen the size of the bait I just stole."

There is no taking trout in dry breeches.
Cervantes

Join the Octopus Circus

Octopuses have good memories and can be trained. If you put a crab inside a jar with a loose lid, the octopus will take the top off the jar. You can even play simple games like tug-o-war with an octopus. They also seem to like to be stroked. Have you petted your octopus today?

If a man sits all day on the shore of a lake with a pole in his hand, people call him a patient fisherman. If the same man sits on his porch at home thinking things over, people call him that lazy man down the street.

Why were the little trout thrown out of the school?

They were always playing cod tricks.

Give a man a fish and he eats for a day.
Teach a man how to fish,
and he eats for a lifetime.
Abraham Lincoln

"That's not really what I meant by cleaning him."

© 2002 Jonny Hawkins

A Whale of a Story

The largest fish is the whale shark. It can grow to a length of 41 feet and weigh up to 16.5 tons.

Two men were fishing on one of the big lakes behind one of the large dams on the Missouri River. Accidentally, one of the men dropped his wallet over the side of the boat.

Two weeks later one of the men was back fishing with another friend. All of a sudden they saw a carp jump out of the water with the same wallet that had been lost two weeks previously.

The carp tossed the wallet to another carp that emerged from the water. This went on repeatedly until the last carp tossed the wallet into the boat of the fishermen.

One of the fishermen remarked, "This is the first time I've ever seen carp to carp walleting."

What did the fish say to the cat?
Sorry, I can't stay for dinner.

What is the best way to raise a whale?
Use a crane.

What is the best way to catch a school of
  fish?
With a bookworm.

Do Fish Spit?

You bet they do, and you had better watch out! The yellow-and-black banded archerfish are sure shots. They live near riverbanks in Thailand and lurk in the water near various plants. The archerfish waits for an unsuspecting insect to come along and land on one of the plants. It then spits water in a semiautomatic hunting method at the insect. The spit knocks the insect into the water, which provides a meal for the archerfish. The longest recorded spit for an archerfish is five feet.

How can you tell when there is a whale under your bed?

When your head hits the ceiling.

Dogfish in Tennessee are very big and mean. In fact, some people report that they've seen two of them tree a bear.

A minister was watching a young boy fishing in a lake. The minister said to the young man, "Do you read your Bible?"

"Oh, yes, sir," replied the boy.

"Young man, do you know any of the parables?" asked the minister.

"Oh, yes, sir," replied the boy.

"Which one do you like the best?"

The boy looked up and said with a smile, "I like the parable where everybody loafs and fishes."

Noah fishes for rainbow trout.

© 2002 Jonny Hawkins

What did the bus driver say to the fish?
What school do you go to?

Get Out Your Maps

Salmon usually take a round trip journey
of 700 miles through the Pacific Ocean to
the Queen Charlotte Islands of British
Columbia before they return to spawn.

Mrs. Cod: Why aren't you swimming home,
little fish?

Sardine: I'm staying for the after-school
program.

First fisherman: What is yellow, smooth,
and very dangerous?

Second fisherman: I give up.

First fisherman: Shark-infested custard.

What do you say to a crying whale?
Quit your blubbering.

How did Jonah feel when the great fish swallowed him?

Down in the mouth.

Where Did the Arms Go?

How many arms does a starfish have? They usually have 5. If they lose one they can grow a new one in its place. If a starfish is cut in half, each half will become a new starfish. Some starfish have as many as 40 arms.

A fishing enthusiast thinks that fish should bite on a fancy lure just because he did.

Quin Ryan

Why did the guppy join the army's motor-ized division?

It wanted to be in a fish tank.

"The Tri-Angler"

© 2002 Jonny Hawkins

Customer: Waiter, there's a piece of canvas in my fish.

Waiter: Of course, sir. You ordered sailfish.

The True Sport Fisherman

© 2002 Jonny Hawkins

What do you say when you want to stop a
   fishing boat?

Whoa, whoa, whoa the boat.

Old Big Mouth

The mouth of the blue whale is 20 feet
wide. A 90-ton blue whale can eat up to 4
tons of zooplankton a day.

A young boy was on his way home when
he saw the local preacher walking toward
him. The boy realized that it was Sunday
and that he had been fishing during
church time.

As they drew closer together, the
young boy smiled and held out a string of
catfish. "Reverend, see what these
catfish got for biting worms on a Sunday?

What did Jonah say when asked how he
   was feeling?

Very whale, thank you.

Did you hear about the man who quit going fishing on Sundays and started going to church? The minister began to notice him as he became a regular attendee.

The minister said, "Walter, it is good to see you and your wife here every Sunday."

Walter responded, "Well, parson, I figured I'd rather hear your sermon than hers."

Do Fish Sweat?

People have asked the question: "Do fish sweat?" Fish do something similar to sweating. Saltwater fish take on a lot of salt from the water they swim in. Because of this, they have to get rid of the excess salt. With the aid of special "salt cells" they put back into the water the excess salt they do not use.

First fisherman: What fish only swims at night?

Second fisherman: You've got me guessing.

First fisherman: A starfish.

What does a father whale say to a young
   whale after reading it a story before
   bed?

All's whale that ends whale.

Customer: Waiter, do you have any
   lobster tails?

Waiter: Of course, sir. Once upon a time,
   there was a little lobster...

© 2002 Jonny Hawkins

*I continually read of men who said
they could be just as happy not
catching trout as catching them. To me,
that even then sounded pious nonsense,
and rather more of an excuse than a
statement of fact. . . .No, I want to get
them, and every time I slip on a wader,
and put up a fly, it is with this in mind.*

Brian Clarke

Spread the Fish Tail

The butterfish is found in the Atlantic
coastal waters. It molds its eggs into a
mass that looks like a ball of butter.

What did the psychiatrist say to the
dolphin?

*That'll be $50 for the visit . . . and $300
to dry out the couch.*

The world would be a better place if
people showed as much patience as they
do when they're waiting for a fish to bite.

What do fishing ships eat for breakfast?
Boatmeal.

"That girl has a crush on me.
I wouldn't touch her with a ten-foot pole."

© 2002 Jonny Hawkins

What kind of fish do you eat with peanut
  butter?

Jellyfish.

"Are you sincere or are you just tossing me a line?"

© 2002 Jonny Hawkins

In a Clam Shell

The favorite food of starfish are clams and oysters. The starfish will adhere itself to the shell with tiny suction discs located on its bottom side. It will exert great pressure to open the shell. The clam or oyster will resist with its strong muscle, but it is no contest for the strength and patience of the starfish, who eventually wins the contest. When the clam or oyster finally relaxes its muscle, the starfish moves in and begins to eat it.

Paradise

© 2002 Jonny Hawkins

*Fly-fishing may be a very
pleasant amusement; but angling,
or float-fishing, I can only compare to
a stick and a string, with a worm at one
end and a fool at the other.*

Dr. Samuel Johnson

"You told him that everyday he had to be efficient,
and he thought you said 'afishin'."

© 2002 Jonny Hawkins

A churchgoing father was attempting to teach his son that lying was a sin. He should not lie about anything, even fishing.

The father said, "Do you know what happens to fishermen who lie when they die?"

The boy responded, "I guess they lie still."

If fishing interferes with your business, give up your business. . . . The trout do not rise in Greenwood Cemetery.
Sparse Grey Hackle

How do you get a dolphin out of a can?
Get a can opener.

The Four-Eyed Fish

The anabelps is a four-eyed fish. The eyes are divided into two parts. The top half of each eye looks at objects above the surface; the bottom half of the eye sees underwater objects.

What type of fish play Crazy 8s?
Card sharks.

Where do fish wash themselves?
In Basstubs.

"Hold it! It might be the latest fish finder!"

© 2002 Jonny Hawkins

How did the robber fish escape from the police after they robbed the river-bank?

They drove the getaway carp.

Why don't fish play tennis?

They might get caught in the net.

Huff and Puff and Blow Your Life Away

One of the most dangerous fish in the ocean is the puffer fish. Its poison is 275 times more deadly than cyanide. The Japanese consider the puffer fish a rare delicacy. They call it *fugu*.

Fugu dinners will sell up to $150 a plate. Death by the puffer fish is not pleasant. First you feel a tingling in your lips and mouth. Then your fingers go numb. Your entire body begins to be paralyzed. You cannot talk or move, and, eventually, you stop breathing. Death usually follows in a few minutes—or if you are strong you might last up to six hours. There is no known antidote for this dangerous toxin. This danger doesn't slow down the Japanese. They consume around $50 million worth of fugu a year.

Mr. Tuna: Those sea mollusks told me you swallowed a whole fishing ship. Is that true?

Mr. Whale: Ah, that's just a bunch of abalone.

I used to go fishing until one day it struck me: You can buy fish. What am I doing in a boat at 4:30 in the morning? If I want a hamburger, I don't track cattle down.

Kenny Rogerson

Customer: Do you have any cockroaches?

Bait shop owner: Yes, we sell them to fishermen.

Customer: I would like 20,000 of them.

Bait shop owner: Why do you want 20,000 cockroaches? That will catch a lot of fish.

Customer: It is not for fish. I'm moving tomorrow, and my lease says I must leave my apartment in the condition in which I found it.

Big-Time Lobster

The largest lobster ever caught was a North Atlantic lobster. On February 11, 1997, off the coast of Nova Scotia, Canada, a lobster weighing 44 pounds and six ounces was pulled from the sea. This lobster was measured at three feet six inches from the tail to the largest claw.

Catfishing

© 2002 Jonny Hawkins

First fish: Do whales have big noses on their backs?

Second fish: No, they don't.

First fish: Oh, no! I must have fallen in love with a submarine.

Give a man a fish and he eats for a day.
Teach him how to fish and you
get rid of him for the whole weekend.
Zenna Schaffer

Simon Peter saith unto them,
I go a fishing.
They say unto him,
We also go with thee.
John 21:3

What kind of fish is the most stupid?
Simple salmon.

First fisherman: What kind of fish can't keep a secret?

Second fisherman: That's a mystery.

First fisherman: A large-mouth bass.

Big-Time Minnow

The Colorado squawfish is technically a minnow. However, some squawfish have been caught weighing over 100 pounds and measuring up to 6 feet in length.

Angling: The name given to fishing by people who can't fish.
Stephen Leacock

First fisherman: Do fish perspire?

Second fisherman: You've got me.

First fisherman: Of course they do. What do you think makes the sea so salty?

What sea creature is both small and large
  at the same time?

Jumbo shrimp.

What is the difference between a tuna
  fish and a piano?

You can't tune a fish.

"Your wife won't let you get away
to the lake this weekend?"

*Every day I see the head of the largest
trout I ever hooked, but did not land.*

Theodore Gordon

Talk About a Sting

The sting of a box jellyfish or sea wasp causes almost instant death. This creature lives off the shores of Australia and has one of the most potent poisons. After being stung, a person gasps for breath, develops an extreme temperature, and dies.

In Wilbur's mind,
he was teaching the *fish* a lesson.

How do you catch an electric eel?
With a lightning rod.

A man from the city went fishing on a backwoods pond with a farmer friend. Time after time the city man would bait his hook with a worm. And time after time the fish would steal the worm off the hook.

The man from the city turned to his farmer friend and said, "Isn't that something . . . the way they get the worms?"

The farmer responded, "Ain't so amazing. They do it for a living."

A man who fishes habitually for carp has a strange look in his eyes.
Arthur Ransome

Watch Out, Captain Nemo!

The largest recorded squid was washed ashore in New Zealand. It was 70 feet long, weighed well over a ton, and had an eye 16 inches across.

How would you like to have a 16-inch eye looking at you?

The suckers on a 50-foot squid are about four inches across. Some sperm whales have been found with 18-inch sucker scars on them. Scientists estimate that to make a scar this big, the squid would have to be 200 feet in length.

First fisherman: I've got a secret to share, and you must not tell anyone.

Second fisherman: I especially wouldn't tell a large-mouth bass.

First fisherman: You've got to keep this quiet.

Second fisherman: Okay, I won't tell a sole.

First fisherman: I don't want you to tell any fish.

Second fisherman: Okay, I won't tell a shoal.

There's a fine line between fishing and standing on the shore looking like an idiot.
Steven Wright

How do you get a dolphin out of a
    Jell-O box?
Read the directions on the back.

"What pound test line you usin'?"

© 2002 Jonny Hawkins

Even Whales Get Lost

In 1985, a whale entered San Francisco Bay under the Golden Gate Bridge. It proceeded up the busy shipping lanes into the Sacramento–San Joaquin River Delta. For 25 days the Pacific humpback wandered in the delta area. The newspapers called the whale "Humphrey." The whale finally made it back to the ocean, but returned to the bay on several occasions to visit. Humphrey was last spotted in 1990.

What is King Arthur's favorite fish
to eat?

Swordfish.

First fisherman: Why did King Neptune
go to the doctor's office?

Second fisherman: That's a mystery
to me.

First fisherman: He had a herring
problem.

Why did Ms. Shark kiss the ocean marker?

Because it was her lover buoy.

First fisherman: Why did the whale cross
the ocean?

Second fisherman: I have no idea.

First fisherman: To get to the other tide.

Happy Birthday

The age of fish can be determined by looking at their scales. The scales have growth rings similar to trees. Some people measure the number of rings on the ear bone.

Claude works for the government in an extremely sensitive capacity.

© 2002 Jonny Hawkins

A family sat down for dinner with a guest at the table. The young son said, "Mother, isn't this roast beef we're eating?"

"Yes, it is. Why do you ask?" said the mother.

"Well, I thought I heard daddy say he was going to bring home a big fish tonight."

What fish warms the earth?

The sunfish.

*You can always tell a fisherman,
but you can't tell him much.*
Corey Ford

Exceeding the Speed Limit

The fastest swimming fish is the cosmopolitan sailfish. It has been clocked swimming more than 60 miles an hour for short distances. The bluefin tuna can swim up to 43 miles an hour. Yellowfin tuna have been clocked at short bursts of speed up to 47 miles per hour. Flying fish can travel up to 40 miles per hour, and dolphins swim at 37 miles per hour. The best that humans can do is close to 15 miles per hour.

> *To live is not necessary.*
> *To fish is necessary.*
> Latin inscription

A fisherman from the city was out fishing on a lake in a small boat. He noticed another man in a small boat open his tackle box and take out a mirror. Being curious the man rowed over and asked, "What is the mirror for?"

"That's my secret way to catch fish," said the other man. "Shine the mirror on the top of the water. The fish notice the spot of sun on the water above and they swim to the surface. Then I just reach down and net them and pull them into the boat."

"Wow! Does that really work?"

"You bet it does."

"Would you be interested in selling that mirror? I'll give you $25 for it."

"Well, okay."

After the money was transferred, the city fisherman asked, "By the way, how many fish have you caught this week?"

"You're the sixth."

"It looks like a dogfish to me."

© 1999 Jonny Hawkins

There was a young fellow named Fisher,
Who was fishing for fish in a fissure,
When a cod, with a grin,
Pulled the fisherman in;
Now they're fishing the fissure for
    Fisher.

"The worms are under the fried chicken."

© 2002 Jonny Hawkins

Labor Pains

The female sea horse lays her eggs in the male's pouch. It is there that the sea horses are hatched and grow until the male goes into labor and expels the young into the sea. These birth contractions can last for several hours.

A friend was visiting his fishing buddy when he noticed a large fish mounted and hanging on a wall. Under the fish was a sign that read: IF I HAD KEPT MY MOUTH SHUT I WOULDN'T BE HERE.

How does an octopus go to war?
Fully armed.

Some of the 10-inch crappies caught in the pond last summer are now six feet long.

First fisherman: What stupid white whale bumps into a lot of ships?

Second fisherman: I give up.

First fisherman: Moby Jerk.

"I don't like eating carp all that much, but it fills the bill."

© 2002 Jonny Hawkins

Coconut Hunters

The purse crab lives on islands in the southwest Pacific and the Indian Ocean. It can grow to be 18 inches long. This relative of the hermit crab climbs coconut palms and snips off young coconuts. It then returns to the ground to eat them.

Mr. Cod: How do I become a flying fish?
Mr. Fluke: Join a flight school.

What do little fish watch on weekends?
Saturday morning carptoons.

Going fishing gives you a lot of exercise. You have to stretch your arms to their full length every time you meet a friend to show them the size of fish that got away.

A fisherman's wife was hoping to get her husband's fanatic interest in fishing diverted. She surprised him on his birthday by getting him a king-size waterbed. He had it stocked with trout.

Look, Ma, I'm Flying

Flying fish actually do not fly. They glide through the air. As they leave the water their tail gives an extra flip to help increase their speed of takeoff. Flying fish have been clocked at speeds of 20 miles per hour. They have been known to travel as far as 1,300 feet in one glide through the air.

It has been said that the very thoughtful wife is the one who has some steaks in the freezer when her husband returns from a fishing trip.

I caught a fish so big that the Polaroid picture weighed 12 pounds.

"So that's where fish sticks come from."

© 2002 Jonny Hawkins

It was a fine way to spend the day—
wading in a favorite trout stream after
placing several hooks into deep, dark
pools. The only problem was that the man
was playing golf.

"It's my way of vacationing.
I'm a commercial fisherman."

© 2002 Jonny Hawkins

Teacher: If I give you five goldfish today and seven goldfish tomorrow, how many will you have?

Student: Fourteen.

Teacher: How do you figure that?

Student: I already have two goldfish.

That's Big

The world record for brook trout is 14.5 pounds. This fish was caught in the Nipigon River of Lake Superior.

Carl and Stuart loved to go fishing together. One day a problem arose. Stuart caught his limit; Carl didn't even get a bite. Carl thought it must be dumb luck on Stuart's part.

The second day, Stuart barely got his line in the water when he caught a large trout. It wasn't long before Stuart again had his limit of fish, but Carl caught nothing.

On the third day Carl thought he would try fishing by himself. An hour before dawn he snuck out to the lake alone. After about an hour of fishing—trying different types of bait—he felt a tug on his line. With great excitement Carl reeled in the line. As the hook came out of the water he noticed there was a sign attached to it. It read, "Where's Stuart?"

A fellow isn't thinking mean—out fishing.

His thoughts are mostly clean—out fishing.

He doesn't knock his fellowmen

Or harbor any grudges then.

A fellow's at his finest when—out fishing.

The rich are comrades to the poor—out fishing.

All brothers of a common core—out fishing.

The urchin with the pin and string

Can chum with millionaire and king.

Vain pride is a forgotten thing—out fishing.

A feller's glad to be a friend—out fishing.

A helpful hand he'll always lend—out fishing.

The brotherhood of rod and line,

And sky and stream is always fine.

Men come real close to God's design—out fishing.

Fish with the Wandering Eye

Flatfish are born with two eyes—one on each side of their heads. However, as they grow older, one eye slowly moves and grows over to the other side of the head. This is a good adaptation since flatfish spend most of their time lying on their sides, burying themselves in the sand. As they lie in the sand both eyes are looking for a good meal to come by.

Mama fish: Don't bite that hook!

Small fry: Why not?

Mama fish: You're too young to face the reel world.

Redefining "Commercial Fisherman"

© 2002 Jonny Hawkins

What kind of fish has perfect pitch?
A piano tuna.

We have changed chairman to chairperson. Should we change fisherman to fisherperson?

The True Fishing Fish

The angler fish has a long fin that grows like a fishing pole and hangs in front of its head. At the end of this growth is a luminous growth. This growth wiggles like worms to attract prey.

As the prey is drawn to the angler's "fishing pole," the fish darts forward and swallows its meal.

There ain't but one time to go fishin' and that's whenever you can.
Diron Talbert

Patient: Doctor, every bone in my body hurts.
Doctor: Be glad you're not a herring.

*The literature of angling
falls into genres:
the instructional and the devotional.
The former is written by fishermen who
write, the latter by writers who fish.*

William Humphrey

One Big Gulp

Gulper fish live deep in the sea and can
grow to be as big as six feet in length. They
have a whiplike tail, but most of their
body is just one big mouth ready to swallow prey.

Why didn't the shark have to pay cash at
the checkout counter?

He had a credit cod with him.

A man and his wife were in a boat on a
lake. While the man fished, his wife read
a book while shading herself with an
umbrella.

The game warden motored up. "Don't you know this is a private lake?" the warden asked the man. "It would be breaking the law to take any fish from here."

"Actually, officer," the wife intervened, "for him, it would be miraculous."

Why do whales never lie?
The ocean floor isn't very comfortable.

A rich kid from the city went to summer camp. At camp they gave him a fishing pole and some bait. He tossed his line into the water and sat there for about a minute.

He then threw his pole down and walked away. One of the other children asked him what was wrong. The rich kid replied, "I just can't seem to get waited on."

Talk About a Head Trip

The kurtus from Australia incubates its eggs on its forehead.

I cannot imagine anyone writing a whole book about maggots, whereas many a man has spent much of his life thinking and writing about a fisherman's flies.

Arthur Ransome

How can you tell there is a dolphin in the refrigerator?

You can see his flipper marks in the cheesecake.

The fishing business is simple. All you have to do is get there yesterday when the fish were biting.

First fisherman: Why didn't the other actors like working with the whale?

Second fisherman: I have no idea.

First fisherman: He was always spouting off.

First fisherman: What do you get if you cross a shark with a parrot?

Second fisherman: Who knows?

First fisherman: An animal that talks your head off.

"You don't really have dry skin.
The scales are because you have
spent too much time fishing."

© 2002 Jonny Hawkins

Loyalty

Sperm whales have strong family ties. Parent whales of a sick or wounded calf will help it stay at water level so it can breathe until it recovers or dies. Female sperm whales that have been harpooned have been seen held above the water by male whales. Whalers knew of this loyalty and used it to kill the male whales.

Which side of the fish has the most scales?

The outside.

Whale: Why did the dolphins paint their flippers red?

Walrus: I don't know. Why?

Whale: So they could hide in the strawberry patch.

Whale: Did you ever see a dolphin in a strawberry patch?

Walrus: No!

Whale: That proves it works.

I firmly believe that if the whole material medicia, as now used, could be sunk to the bottom of the sea, it would be all the better for mankind—and all the worse for the fishes.

Oliver Wendell Holmes

Which sharks don't get cavities?

Those that use toothpaste.

"That's hardly sporting, Caldwell!"

© 2001 Jonny Hawkins

The Underwater Bodyguard

The hermit crab lives in a shell on which a sea anemone often rides as a bodyguard. The stinging tentacles of the sea anemone help ward off predators and protect the crab. In turn, the sea anemone gets a free ride around the ocean to new areas for food. When the hermit crab changes shells it taps on its present shell letting the sea anemone know they are changing homes. The anemone will let go of the old shell and the hermit crab will move it with its claw to its new shell.

Hunting and fishing are the second and third oldest professions, yet bonefishing is the only sport that I know of, except perhaps swordfishing, that combines hunting and fishing.

Stanley M. Babson

First fisherman: What is in the sea and is also on your arm?

Second fisherman: I don't have the foggiest.

First fisherman: A mussel.

Why were the sardines out of work?
Because they got canned.

What do you get when you cross a saber
tooth tiger with a shark?
A very nervous mailman.

Swim As Fast As You Can

There are approximately 354 species of known sharks. It is estimated that two-thirds of a shark's brain is used in connection with smelling. They can sense the odor of blood one quarter of a mile away. They can hear a struggling fish or a human swimmer more than a mile away.

© 2001 Jonny Hawkins

A Tombstone in England

Here lies poor Thompson, all alone,
As dead and cold as any stone.
In wading in the River Nith
He took a cold, which stopp'd his breath.
He fish'd the stream for ten years past,
Death caught him in his net at last.

Why should a fisherman always be
wealthy?

Because all his business is net profit.

Fish gain weight slowly—except the one
that got away.

Touch an Octopus and Die

The beautiful blue-ringed octopus lives in
the tropical waters near Australia and
Indonesia. Its bite is very dangerous for
humans. It injects its victim with a large
dose of the same poison found in puffer fish.
This toxin can kill a human in a few hours.

First fisherman: What kind of whale
   flies?
Second fisherman: Tha's above my head.
First fisherman: A pilot whale.

Why can't dolphins fly?
They don't have propellers.

© 2000 Jonny Hawkins

Why did the whale cross the road?
To prove he wasn't chicken.

A fisherman is the only person who tells a
lie with his arms stretched out.

Why did the dolphin swim on his back?
So he wouldn't get his tennis shoes wet.

Tiny Dolphins

The smallest sea mammal is the Commerson's dolphin. It weighs between 50 and 70 pounds.

*There is nothing that attracts human
nature more powerfully than the sport of
tempting the unknown with a fishing line.*
Henry van Dyke

What newspaper do fish in the sea read?
The Scaly News.

First fisherman: What kind of food
    improves your vision?
Second fisherman: That's a hard one.
First fisherman: Seefood.

"You ought to take the worm *out* of it first."

© 2002 Jonny Hawkins

What should you do if you find Jaws in
the bathtub?
Pull out the plug!

Light in the Darkness

In the deepest oceans there are fish that
have luminous lights. These lights seem to
attract prey and are also signals used for
mating. Indian ocean fish have a large spot
under each eye that glows. The bathy-
sphere fish has pale blue glowing spots on
its sides. It also has lights in its teeth to
attract prey. The hatchet fish has greenish
lights that resemble teeth. Instead of
attracting prey it does the opposite—it
scares off enemies.

What would you be if a shark was in your
bathtub?
Chicken of the sea.

How do you divide the sea in half?
With a sea saw.

What did the little lobster get on its
   math test?

Sea-plus.

What did the little lobster get on its math test?

Who performs operations at the fish
   hospital?

The head sturgeon.

© 2002 Jonny Hawkins

How do oysters get ready for work?

They wake up pearly in the morning.

A Whale of a Long Time

A fin whale can live for 116 years.

A killer whale can live for 90 years.

A blue whale can live for 45 years.

A sperm whale can live for 32 years.

A white or beluga whale can live for 17 years.

How do eels get out of a muddy seabed?
With their 4-eel dive.

What is the best name for the wife of a
   fisherman?
Nettie.

Where do jellyfish sleep?
In tentacles.

What lives in the ocean, is grouchy, and
   hates neighbors?
A hermit crab.

Where do you find a down-and-out
   octopus?
On squid row.

The Great White Shark

There are 354 species of sharks. They range in length from 6 inches to 49 feet. Of the different species of sharks, 35 have been known to attack man. There are approximately 12 species that attack people on a regular basis. The one feared the most is the great white shark. The largest of the predatory fish, it can get up to 20 feet long and weigh as much as 5,000 pounds.

"I told you not to bait those hooks."

© 2002 Jonny Hawkins

Where do sea horses sleep?
In barnacles.

What's the most exact body of water?
The Specific Ocean.

"It'd be cheaper if you just stocked it with bass."

© 1995 Jonny Hawkins

Why does Neptune wear a tank top?
To show off his mussels.

What kind of bed does a baby fish sleep in?
A bassinet.

First fisherman: Have you ever seen a
   man-eating fish?
Second fisherman: Sure.
First fisherman: Where was that?
Second fisherman: In a seafood restaurant.

Underwater Nests

The male three-spined stickleback builds
a nest for the young fish to be hatched in.
He does this by collecting pieces of various aquatic plants. He then glues them
together with a "cement" secretion from
his kidneys. He makes a small underwater
pit, a burrow, and then the female lays her
eggs in it.

What kind of bed do oysters sleep in?
A waterbed.

"Ah yes...sitting ducks."

© 2002 Jonny Hawkins

Why is the sea measured in knots?

Because of the ocean tide.

How did Robinson Crusoe survive after his boat sank?

He used a bar of soap and washed himself ashore.

What did the young whale do when his mother told him to go to bed?

He blubbered.

Who stays with young squids when their parents go out?

Babysquidders.

Why was the crab crabby when he woke up?

The sea snore kept him awake all night.

Why do fish have such huge phone bills?

When they get on the line they can't get off.

Do you know what they call a grouchy person at the beach?

A sand crab.

Why don't fish go near computers?

They don't want to get caught in the Internet.

What do you call a fish with two legs?
A two-knee fish.

"Maybe we need an entertainment center."

© 1992 Jonny Hawkins

Rules for Avoiding Sharks

1. Don't swim alone.
2. Don't swim with an open wound.
3. Don't swim at night or in dirty water.
4. Don't stay in the water when a shark is spotted.
5. Don't grab an injured shark.

What did the shrimp yell when he got caught in the seaweed?

Kelp! Kelp!

What song do fish sing to each other?

Salmonchanted Evening.

First fisherman: You don't know anything about music. What is a scale?

Second fisherman: A scale is a feather on a fish.

First fisherman: Fish don't have feathers.

Second fisherman: How about flying fish?

Where did the whale go when it was almost bankrupt?
It went to see the loan shark.

Floating Fish

What causes fish to turn upside down and float to the surface of the water when they die? After death their body begins to decompose. This process causes gases that collect in the internal organs like the stomach. As the gases build up it causes the fish to turn upside down and float to the surface of the water.

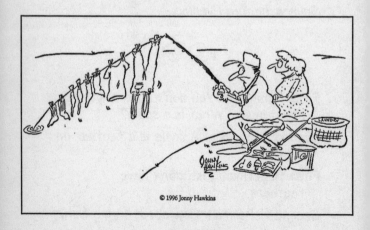

© 1996 Jonny Hawkins

*The curious thing about fishing
is you never want to go home.
If you catch anything, you can't stop.
If you don't catch anything,
you hate to leave in case
something might bite.*
Gladys Taber

Who are all the fish in the sea afraid of?
Jack the Kipper.

Where do king crabs live?
In sand castles.

What did the boy octopus say to the girl
   squid?
*I want to hold your hand, hand, hand,
   hand...*

"Yup. They're biting."

© 1996 Jonny Hawkins

Do Fish Drink?

Have you ever wondered if fish drink water? The answer is yes and no. Yes, they do take on water in two primary ways. The first is through a process called "osmosis." Some water enters the fish through tiny holes in their skin. They also take on some water when they swallow their food. However, fish do not drink water in the same sense as mammals do when they are thirsty.

What is a fish's favorite game show?
Name That Tuna.

What happened to the man who caught an electric eel?
He was shocked.

Where do fish wash up?
In the basstub.

What should you do for a deaf fish?
Get a herring aid.

Who was Jonah's tutor?
The fish that brought him up.

That's a Mouthful

The Mozambique mouthbreeder females carry their fertilized eggs in their mouths. The baby fish, after hatching, remain in the mouth until they have absorbed their egg yolks. The small fish then venture out for small distances, but they return for safety. This lasts up to five weeks. The parent fish will not eat anything during this time to keep from swallowing the young.

How did the fish that swallowed Jonah obey the divine law?

Jonah was a stranger, and he took him in.

First fisherman: Have you ever seen a catfish?

Second fisherman: Of course.

First fisherman: How did he hold the pole?

Other Books by Bob Phillips

The All-New Clean Joke Book

Awesome Good Clean Jokes for Kids

The Best of the Good Clean Jokes

A Classic Collection of Golf Jokes and Quotes

Controlling Your Emotions Before They Control You

Dude, Got Another Joke?

Extremely Good Clean Jokes for Kids

How Can I Be Sure?

Over the Hill & On a Roll

Over the Next Hill & Still Rolling

Super Cool Jokes and Games for Kids

So You Want to Be a Bible Trivia Expert?

Super-Duper Good Clean Jokes for Kids

Totally Cool Clean Jokes for Kids

The World's Greatest Collection of Clean Jokes

The World's Greatest Collection of Knock-Knock Jokes for Kids

---

For information on how to purchase any of the above books, contact your local bookstore or send a self-addressed stamped envelope to:

Family Services
P.O. Box 9363
Fresno, California 93702